PRESENTS

THE DEFINITIVE UNOFFICIAL GUIDE TO POKEMON 2026

A TOTALLY INDEPENDENT PUBLICATION

Written by Naomi Berry
Designed by Chris Dalrymple

A Pillar Box Red Publication

© 2025. Published by Pillar Box Red Publishing Limited. Printed in Romania.

Pillar Box Red Publishing Ltd., 25 Herbert Place, Dublin, D02 AY86. info@pillarboxredpublishing.co.uk

This is a 100% unofficial and independent publication, the inclusion of any logos, images, quotes and references does not imply endorsement. Whilst every care has been taken in researching and writing this book, due to the nature of the subject matter, some information may change over time. It has no connection with any organisation(s), personality, or personalities associated with The Pokémon Company, or Pokémon games, or with any organisation or individual connected in any way whatsoever with the organisation(s) or personality or personalities featured.

Whilst every effort has been made to ensure the accuracy of information within this publication, the publisher shall have no liability to any person or entity with respect to any inaccuracy, misleading information, loss or damage caused directly or indirectly by the information contained within this book.

Pokémon is a registered trademark of The Pokémon Company, Nintendo, Game Freak and Creatures Inc. All screenshots shown in this guide were taken from Pokémon, a game created and published by The Pokémon Company, Nintendo, Game Freak and Creatures Inc. This is a 100% unofficial and independent guide, which is in no way licensed, authorised or endorsed by or otherwise connected in any way with Pokémon or The Pokémon Company, Nintendo, Game Freak and Creatures Inc., or any other individuals from The Pokémon Company, Nintendo, Game Freak and Creatures Inc. and authors of Pokémon. All copyrights and trademarks are recognised and used specifically for the purpose of criticism, review and reportage.

The views expressed are solely those of the author and do not reflect the opinions of Pillar Box Red Publishing Limited. All rights reserved.

ISBN 978-1-917522-17-5

Images © The Pokémon Company, Nintendo, Game Freak and Creatures Inc.
Cover Image © Alamy / DarkBarrios

CONTENTS

- WELCOME + POKEDEX ENTRY 6-7
- DO YOU SPEAK POKEMON? 8-13
- THE WORLD OF POKEMON 14-17
- POKEMON TYPES 101 18-23
- A TIMELINE OF EVOLUTION 24-29
- POKEMON GO! 30-31
- LEGENDARY CROSSWORD 32
- WHO'S THAT POKEMON? I 33
- SPOT THE DIFFERENCE I 34
- BATTLE QUIZ 35
- POKEDEX PECULIARITIES 36-37
- KNOW THY ENEMY 38-39
- NEWLY NEFARIOUS 40
- ROGUE ROLL CALL 41
- BEST IN CLASS 42-43
- MAZE MISSION 44
- WHO'S THAT POKEMON? II 45
- WHOLESOME BEHAVIOUR 46
- DEEP SEA SEARCH 47
- SPOT THE DIFFERENCE II 48
- SANDS SCRAMBLE 49
- PIKACHU PROFILE 50-51

THE CREATOR: ARCEUS 52
BATTLE CHEAT SHEET 53
POKEMON FUN FACTS 54-55
UP CLOSE & PERSONAL 56-57
POKEMON TCG 58-59
THE BIG POKEMON QUIZ 60-61
ANSWERS 62-63

WELCOME

Hello there, aspiring Pokemon trainer! Welcome to the wonderful world of Pokemon!

You're about to embark on an amazing journey, and this guide will be your trusted companion. Whether you're just starting out or you're already a seasoned trainer, there's something here for everyone who dreams of becoming a Pokemon Champion.

In these pages, you'll master essential terminology, explore diverse regions from Kanto to Galar, and learn the type matchups that separate good trainers from great ones. Discover the timeline of Pokemon history, meet iconic starter Pokemon, and uncover amazing facts that might surprise even experienced trainers. Test your knowledge with champion-level quizzes or unwind with fun puzzles.

Remember, the bond between trainer and Pokemon is built on knowledge and understanding. So grab your Pokedex and let's begin this incredible journey together!

Your Pokemon adventure starts now. Are you ready to catch 'em all? Great! Let's start by filling out your player profile card...

POKEDEX ENTRY

TRAINER CARD

Name:

Age:

Hometown:

Favourite Pokemon:

Favourite Type:

Favourite Pokemon Game:

DO YOU SPEAK POKEMON?

Ever hear a Trainer talk about HMs, PP, or STAB and wonder if they're speaking another language? Don't worry - you're not alone! The world of Pokemon is packed with special terms, battle lingo, and abbreviations that might sound confusing at first. But once you crack the code, you'll start thinking (and battling!) like a real pro.

This A-to-Z glossary is your one-stop shop for all things Poké-talk. Sure, you may know what a gym is in your world, but a Poké-specific Gym (yeah, clock the capital G) is a very different entity (much less sweaty, for sure). Curious about what Held Items actually do? Don't quite know the difference between Legendary and Mythical? We've got you.

ABILITY

Each Pokemon has a special passive skill that affects them in battle. Not all abilities are made equal - some are advantageous (like Intimidate, Huge Power and Tinted Lens), and others are literally awful (like Truant, Truant and... oh! Truant). Most Pokemon only have one ability, but some lucky critters can take on two. And once an ability is set, it's locked in for life - unless the Pokemon evolves out of it.

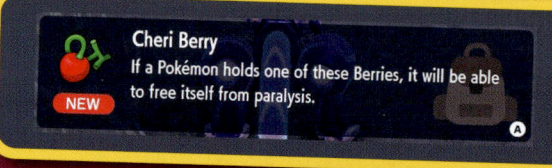

BERRIES

Berries are small fruits that are common Held Items for Pokemon. They have a wide variety of healing and restoration effects - from curing poison and restoring PP to increasing friendship and halving damage taken. Small, but mighty.

BST

This stands for Base Stat Total, the combined number you get when you add up all six of a Pokemon's base stats: HP, Attack, Defense, Special Attack, Special Defense, and Speed.

Did you know that Zygarde is the only Pokemon with two regular Abilities, but no Hidden Ability at all?

CORE SERIES

The main series of Pokemon Games, grouped by Generations. This line-up includes Red, Blue and Yellow (Gen I); Gold, Silver and Crystal (Gen II); Ruby, Sapphire and Emerald (Gen III); Diamond, Pearl and Platinum (Gen IV); Black and White (Gen V); X and Y (Gen VI); Sun, Moon and Ultra (Gen VII); Sword, Shield and Arceus (VIII); and Scarlet, Violet and Legends Z-A (Gen IX).

DYNAMAX

A special transformation that makes Pokemon grow into literal giants with beefed up stats. First seen in the Galar region (and now in Pokemon GO), Dynamaxing only works in certain spots like stadiums or during Max Raid Battles. It lasts three turns and lets your Pokemon use supercharged attacks called Max Moves.

Congratulations! Your Igglybuff evolved into Jigglypuff!

EGG CYCLE

How long it takes for an egg to hatch. Each egg cycle is around 250 in-game steps (depending on the game), so if a Rattata egg takes 15 cycles to hatch... then do the math (around 3750 steps, if you're wondering).

EVOLUTION

Evolution is when a Pokemon transforms into a new, often stronger form. This can happen when it levels up, uses a special item, or meets certain conditions. Evolved Pokemon usually look different, have better stats, and may even change type or learn new moves. It's one of the main ways to power up your team and fill out your Pokedex.

EGG GROUP

Egg groups decide which Pokemon can breed with each other. If two Pokemon share at least one egg group and are the right genders, they can have an egg. It's how you get baby Pokemon, and sometimes moves they wouldn't learn otherwise.

FRIENDSHIP

Also called happiness, this hidden stat shows how much a Pokemon likes its Trainer. Some Pokemon only evolve when their friendship is high, and certain moves become stronger the more your Pokemon cares about you. You can boost friendship by battling together, using helpful items, or simply going on walks.

> **Eggs and breeding were introduced to the core series game in Gen II. The first Pokemon players could hatch from an egg was Togepi.**

GEN

In Pokemon, a "generation" (Gen) is a set of games introduced together - bringing new regions, new gameplay mechanics, and most importantly, new Pokemon. There have been nine generations so far.

EV

Effort Values (EVs) are hidden points your Pokemon earn by battling, and they help boost specific stats like Attack or Speed. Different opponents give different EVs, and over time, these make your Pokemon stronger than usual. You won't see them directly, but they play a big part in your Pokemon's growth.

GIGANTMAX

A super special version of Dynamaxing that only certain Pokemon can do. Gigantamax Pokemon don't just grow big, they also get a brand-new look and their own unique G-Max Moves.

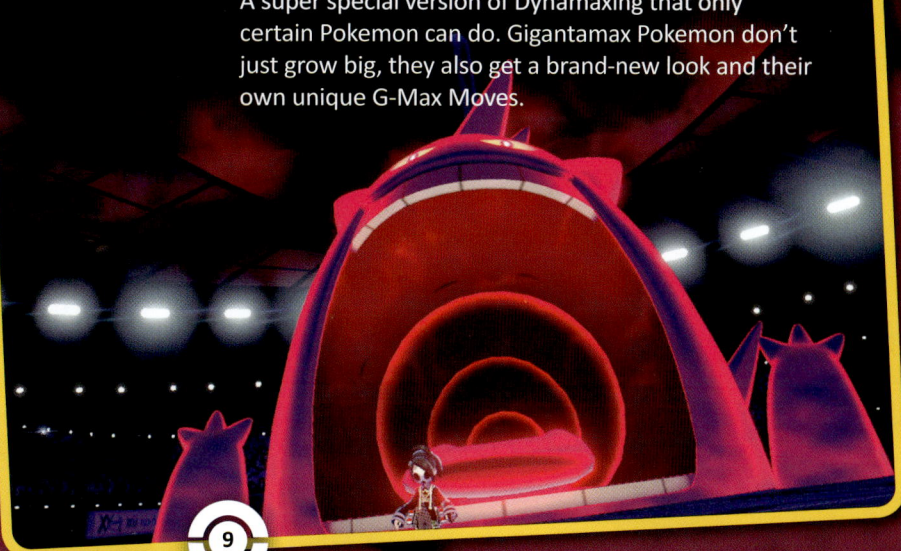

The vast majority of Pokemon that can Gigantamax belong to Gen I or Gen VIII, and Water is the type that has the most Pokemon with Gigantamax forms.

Gen IX added the highest number of Pokemon that don't evolve and aren't Legendary or Mythical: 29 in total. That's way more than Gens IV and VI, which only introduced five each.

HELD ITEM

A held item is something a Pokemon can carry into battle to give it an extra edge. Some heal status problems, boost moves, or power up certain types. The item stays with the Pokemon unless it's used up or removed during the fight.

HM

Hidden Machines (HMs) are special moves you can teach a Pokemon that aren't for battle, but more focused on map navigation in games. Moves like Surf help you cross large seas of water and Cut will slice down any trees standing in your way. Some HMs can be used in battle, but most aren't worth the turn.

HP

Hit Points, essentially a Pokemon's health. When a Pokemon loses all of its HP in battle, it'll faint. HP can be restored at a Pokemon Center, or with certain healing items.

HYPER TRAINING

A training method that allows you to max out a Pokemon's IVs, even if they weren't bred or caught with perfect IVs.

IV

Individual Values (IVs) are hidden numbers that help decide how strong a Pokemon's stats can be. They're set when you catch or receive a Pokemon and range from 0 to 31, with higher numbers being better. IVs make each Pokemon a little different - even ones of the same species.

You are challenged by Gym Leader Katy!

GYM

A place where Pokemon Trainers test their battling skills and help their Pokemon grow stronger. Each Gym usually focuses on a specific type, like Fire or Water. At the top of the Gym is the Gym Leader, the strongest Trainer there and the one you'll need to beat to earn a badge. Taking on Gyms is a key step on the path to becoming a Pokemon Champion.

Gen I is the only generation where its legendary Pokemon (Mewtwo and the birds, Articuno, Zapdos and Moltres) are not involved in the game's main plot.

Fun fact - the most common type for Mythical Pokemon is Psychic.

LEGENDARY

These are rare, powerful Pokemon usually tied to a region's myths or history. Each generation introduces a few, and they often play a key role in the game's story. They're typically one-of-a-kind and boast impressive stats and unique abilities.

LEVEL

A Pokemon's level shows how strong and experienced it is. As Pokemon battle and gain experience, they level up, which improves their stats and lets them learn new moves.

POKEDEX

The Pokedex is a high-tech encyclopedia that records info about every Pokemon you see or catch. Trainers use it to learn about different species and keep track of their progress. It's one of the most important tools on any Pokemon journey.

MEGA EVOLUTION

Mega Evolution is a special transformation some Pokemon can use during battle to become even more powerful. It gives a big boost to their stats, can change their ability, and sometimes even switches up their type.

MYTHICAL

Even rarer than Legendary Pokemon, Mythical Pokemon are surrounded by mystery and often don't appear through normal gameplay. Their existence is sometimes debated in the Pokemon world, and they're usually only available through special events.

POKEMON CENTER

Pokemon Centers are places where Trainers go to heal their Pokemon. They're found in towns and cities and often include spots to trade Pokemon or connect with other players. Think of them as a home base for any Trainer on the go.

PSEUDO-LEGENDARY

This fan-made term refers to super-strong Pokemon that aren't officially Legendary but are just as powerful. They have a total base stat of 600, evolve in three stages, and usually take a while to train. Think of them as the underdog powerhouses of the Pokemon world.

> The OG pseudo-legendary Pokemon from Gen I is the Dratini > Dragonair > Dragonite evolution line. From there, there's been one every generation - though Gen III and Gen VIII had two.

POKE BALL

A Poké Ball is the classic tool Trainers use to catch and carry Pokemon. It's a small, round device that lets you store your Pokemon and call them out when it's battle time. There are all kinds of Poké Balls with special features, but the standard red-and-white one is the most iconic.

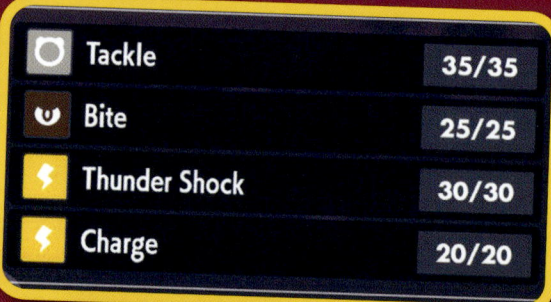

PP

PP stands for Power Points, which show how many times a Pokemon can use a move. Each move has its own PP, and when it runs out, that move can't be used until it's restored. Managing PP is key during long battles or tough journeys.

RAISED

Raised Pokemon float above the ground - either because they're Flying types or have some sort of ability. Since they don't touch the ground, they're safe from Ground-type moves and abilities like Earthquake.

RARE CANDY

A special item that instantly boosts a Pokemon by one level. You can use it on any Pokemon, no matter what level it's at or if it's ready to evolve. It's a handy shortcut when you need a quick power-up!

STATUS EFFECT

A status effect (or status condition) is something that can mess with a Pokemon during battle. It might make them fall asleep, get poisoned, or miss turns. These effects are usually caused by moves and can really change the course of a fight.

TCG

The official acronym for 'Trading Card Game', the Pokemon TCG is just as big as the main series games, with a fresh surge due to the recent popularity of collecting and selling rare cards.

REGION

A region is a specific area in the Pokemon world where each game takes place. Every region has its own landscapes, Pokemon species, and storyline to explore. Think of it like a different country or continent in the Pokemon universe, each with its own adventures to discover.

TM

Stands for 'Technical Machine'. TMs are items that teach Pokemon special moves that they wouldn't be able to learn naturally through experience or evolution.

TYPE

A type is like a Pokemon's element (such as Fire, Water, or Grass etc.) and every Pokemon and move has one (or sometimes two). Types decide which moves are super effective or not very effective. Knowing type matchups is key to winning battles!

> Want to explore the regions of Pokemon? Check out our region chapter on p. 14-17!

SHINY

A shiny Pokemon has a rare and different color from the usual version of its species. They sparkle when they appear and are super hard to find, making them prized by Trainers. Shiny Pokemon don't have better stats - they're just cute.

STAB

Same Type Attack Bonus (STAB) gives a damage boost when a Pokemon uses a move that matches its own type. For example, a Fire-type using a Fire move hits harder thanks to this bonus. It multiplies the move's power by 1.5, making it a smart strategy in battle.

THE WORLD OF POKEMON

From the familiar forests of Kanto to the tropical islands of Alola, each Pokemon region offers its own unique culture, challenges, and creatures to discover.

Every region tells a different story through its landscape, people, and the legendary Pokemon that call it home. Pack your bags, trainers - we're going on the ultimate world tour!

KANTO

- **Starters:** Bulbasaur, Charmander, Squirtle
- **Legendaries:** Articuno, Zapdos, Moltres, Mewtwo, Mew
- **Villains:** Team Rocket

The region that started it all. Based on Japan's Kantō region, this area perfectly captures the essence of suburban Japan with its mix of small towns, bustling cities, and natural landmarks. Kanto's straightforward gym challenge and Team Rocket's schemes created the template that all future regions would follow. The region's design philosophy of "easy to learn, hard to master" became the foundation for the entire Pokemon series.

JOHTO

- **Starters:** Chikorita, Cyndaquil, Totodile
- **Legendaries:** Raikou, Entei, Suicune, Ho-Oh, Lugia, Celebi
- **Villains:** Team Rocket

Inspired by Japan's Kansai region, Johto blends ancient traditions with modern conveniences in perfect harmony. Ancient ruins like the Ruins of Alph and the mystical Tin Tower give Johto a spiritual atmosphere that sets it apart. The post-game return to Kanto doubled the adventure, creating what many consider the ultimate Pokemon experience.

HOENN

- **Starters:** Treecko, Torchic, Mudkip
- **Legendaries:** Kyogre, Groudon, Rayquaza, Regirock, Regice, Registeel, Latios, Latias, Jirachi, Deoxys
- **Villains:** Team Aqua/Magma

This tropical paradise draws inspiration from Japan's Kyushu region, featuring active volcanoes, lush rainforests, and countless water routes. Hoenn's environmental themes of land versus sea feel incredibly relevant today, with Team Aqua and Team Magma's misguided plans threatening ecological disaster. With more water routes than any other region, mastering Surf and Dive became essential for full exploration.

SINNOH

- **Starters:** Turtwig, Chimchar, Piplup
- **Legendaries:** Dialga, Palkia, Giratina, Arceus, Uxie, Mesprit, Azelf, Heatran, Regigigas, Cresselia, Phione, Manaphy, Darkrai, Shaymin
- **Villains:** Team Galactic

Based on Japan's Hokkaido island, Sinnoh is a region of snow-capped mountains, ancient mythology, and underground mysteries. No region takes its legendary Pokemon more seriously - creation myths are woven into every corner, from Team Galactic's cosmic ambitions to the Lake Trio's psychic guardianship. Mount Coronet stands as the region's centerpiece, literally and figuratively connecting all areas while housing the most powerful legendaries.

UNOVA

- **Starters:** Snivy, Tepig, Oshawott
- **Legendaries:** Reshiram, Zekrom, Kyurem, Cobalion, Terrakion, Virizion, Tornadus, Thundurus, Landorus, Victini, Keldeo, Meloetta, Genesect
- **Villains:** Team Plasma

Unova is the first Pokemon region that drew inspiration from somewhere other than Japan. Inspired by New York and the eastern United States, this urban region features everything from bustling metropolises to desert resorts, connected by bridges that span vast bodies of water. The Black 2/White 2 sequels showed how regions could evolve over time, with new areas and updated storylines.

KALOS

- **Starters:** Chespin, Fennekin, Froakie
- **Legendaries:** Xerneas, Yveltal, Zygarde, Diancie, Hoopa, Volcanion
- **Villains:** Team Flare

Bonsoir! This elegant region draws heavy inspiration from France, particularly Paris, with Lumiose City serving as a fashion and culture capital. The region pioneered Mega Evolution and the Fairy type, fundamentally changing competitive battling forever. From the mysterious Azure Bay to the towering Prism Tower, Kalos clearly prioritizes beauty and sophistication in every architectural aspect. Oui oui!

ALOLA

- **Starters:** Rowlet, Litten, Popplio
- **Legendaries:** Solgaleo, Lunala, Necrozma, Tapu Koko, Tapu Lele, Tapu Bulu, Tapu Fini, Magearna, Marshadow, Zeraora
- **Villains:** Team Galactic

Based on Hawaii, Alola is unique in that it has its own Pokemon system, with Island Trials replacing traditional gym battles. This tropical paradise features four distinct islands, each with its own Guardian Deity and unique ecosystem challenges. It also has its own form of Pokemon called Alolan.

GALAR

- **Starters:** Grookey, Scorbunny, Sobble
- **Legendaries:** Zacian, Zamazenta, Eternatus, Kubfu, Urshifu, Regieleki, Regidrago, Glastrier, Spectrier, Calyrex
- **Villains:** Team Yell

Inspired by Great Britain, Galar transforms Pokemon battles into massive sporting events held in packed stadiums. The region's industrial history meets wild countryside, creating diverse environments from the rolling hills of the Wild Area to the urban sprawl of Wyndon. Galar is also home to Dynamax gym battles.

HISUI

- **Starters:** Rowlet, Cyndaquil, Oshawott
- **Legendaries:** Dialga, Palkia, Giratina, Arceus
- **Villains:** Miss Fortunes

Set in ancient Sinnoh before modern civilization, Hisui shows the Pokemon world when humans and Pokemon were still learning to coexist peacefully. This untamed wilderness features harsh conditions where wild Pokemon pose genuine threats to unprepared travelers.

PALDEA

- **Starters:** Sprigatito, Fuecoco, Quaxly
- **Legendaries:** Koraidon, Miraidon
- **Villains:** Team Star

Based on the Iberian Peninsula (Spain, Portugal and Andorra), Paldea features everything from Mediterranean coastlines to snowy mountains, as well as a completely unique anomaly biome: Area Zero. All of the settlements in Paldea are named after food and kitchen related terminology.

POKEMON TYPES 101

Every Pokemon has something special that makes them unique: their type. Think of it like their elemental superpower. Pikachu crackles with electricity because it's Electric-type, while Squirtle loves water because it's a Water-type. But types aren't just about aesthetics - they're the secret to understanding how battles work.

A Pokemon's type determines what moves will hurt them and what moves they can shrug off. Fire beats Grass, Water beats Fire, Grass beats Water - it's nature's way of keeping things balanced. So let's dive in and learn about all eighteen types (yeah, so they got a bit liberal with the definition of 'elements').

GRASS

Nature-loving Pokemon that draw power from the earth and sun. While they might seem gentle, Grass-types can be surprisingly tough in the right hands.

Super Effective Against	Weak To	Resists	Weak Against
Water Ground Rock	Fire Flying Bug Poison Ice	Grass Water Ground Electric	Grass Dragon Steel Bug Fire Flying Poison

WATER

One of the most reliable and popular types, Water Pokemon are known for their balanced stats and wide move pools. Water types are solid all-rounders that can handle most situations, making them perfect for new trainers.

Super Effective Against	Weak To	Resists	Weak Against
Fire Ground Rock	Grass Electric	Steel Water Fire Ice	Water Grass Dragon

FIRE

Fire types are all about raw attacking power and flashy moves. They burn bright and hit hard, though they can sometimes struggle defensively against the wrong matchups.

Super Effective Against	Weak To	Resists	Weak Against
Grass Bug Ice Steel	Water Ground Rock	Fire Grass Ice Steel Fairy Bug	Fire Water Rock Dragon

NORMAL

Don't let the name fool you - Normal types are anything but ordinary. While they don't have any super-effective advantages, they also resist very little, making them unpredictable wildcards.

Super Effective Against	Weak To	Resists	Weak Against
-	Fighting	Ghost	Rock Steel

FIGHTING

The martial artists of the Pokemon world, Fighting-types rely on physical strength and disciplined techniques. They excel at breaking through tough defenses but can struggle against opponents they can't physically touch.

Super Effective Against	Weak To	Resists	Weak Against
Normal Steel Ice Rock Dark	Psychic Fairy Flying	Bug Rock Dark	Poison Flying Psychic Bug Fairy

ELECTRIC

Fast, flashy, and often surprisingly powerful, Electric-types light up any battle. Electric-types are known for their speed and ability to paralyze opponents, though they're not the most defensively minded.

Super Effective Against	Weak To	Resists	Weak Against
Water Flying	Ground	Electric Flying Steel	Grass Electric Ground Dragon

FLYING

Masters of the sky with incredible mobility and grace. Many Flying-types pair with other types, creating diverse combinations that can adapt to different battle strategies while maintaining their signature speed advantage.

Super Effective Against	Weak To	Resists	Weak Against
Fighting Grass Bug	Electric Ice Rock	Fighting Grass Bug	Electric Rock Steel

GROUND

Solid, dependable, and surprisingly powerful, Ground-types are the foundation of many winning teams. Ground-types are excellent at dealing with Electric-types but struggle against anything that can stay airborne.

Super Effective Against	Weak To	Resists	Weak Against
Electric Fire Poison Rock Steel	Water Grass Ice	Poison Rock	Grass Bug

ROCK

Tough as stone and built to last, Rock-types are the ultimate defensive specialists. While Rock-types can take physical hits like champs, they tend to have several common weaknesses that smart opponents will exploit.

Super Effective Against	Weak To	Resists	Weak Against
Fire Ice Flying Bug	Water Grass Fighting Ground Steel	Normal Fire Poison Flying	Fighting Ground Steel

PSYCHIC

The masterminds of the Pokemon world, Psychic-types use mental powers to control the battlefield. These Pokemon often have amazing special attack power and unique abilities, though they can be fragile when faced with more direct approaches.

Super Effective Against	Weak To	Resists	Weak Against
Fighting Poison	Bug Ghost Dark	Fighting Psychic	Psychic Dark Steel

GHOST

Mysterious and otherworldly, Ghost-types play by their own rules. Ghost-types are masters of tricks and status effects, immune to Normal and Fighting moves but vulnerable to their own spooky kind.

Super Effective Against	Weak To	Resists	Weak Against
Psychic Ghost	Ghost Dark	Normal Fighting Poison Bug	Dark

DARK

The rebels and tricksters of the Pokemon world, Dark-types fight dirty and aren't ashamed of it. Dark-types excel at disrupting opponents' strategies and are particularly effective against Psychic-types, though they struggle against Fighting-types' straightforward approach.

Super Effective Against	Weak To	Resists	Weak Against
Psychic Ghost	Fighting Bug Fairy	Psychic Ghost Dark	Fighting Dark Fairy

BUG

Bug-types can be real game-changers in the right situations. While many Bug-types start weak, they often have great potential for growth and some unique tricks up their sleeves.

Super Effective Against	Weak To	Resists	Weak Against
Grass Psychic Dark	Fire Flying Rock	Grass Fighting Ground	Fire Fighting Poison Flying Ghost Steel Fairy

POISON

Sneaky and persistent, Poison-types wear down opponents with status effects. Poison-types might not always win quickly, but they're experts at making their opponents suffer over time.

Super Effective Against	Weak To	Resists	Weak Against
Grass Fairy	Ground Psychic	Grass Fighting Poison Bug Fairy	Poison Ground Rock Ghost Steel

STEEL

The armored knights of the Pokemon world, Steel-types are incredibly difficult to take down. Steel-types resist more attack types than any other, making them excellent team anchors, though they can be slow to finish battles.

Super Effective Against	Weak To	Resists	Weak Against
Ice Rock Fairy	Fire Fighting Ground	Normal Grass Ice Flying Psychic Bug Rock Dragon Steel Fairy	Fire Water Electric Steel

ICE

Beautiful but fragile, Ice-types pack serious offensive punch but struggle to take hits in return. Ice moves are super effective against many types, but Ice-types themselves are vulnerable to common attack types.

Super Effective Against	Weak To	Resists	Weak Against
Grass Ground Flying Dragon	Fire Fighting Rock Steel	Ice	Fire Water Steel

DRAGON

The legendary powerhouses that every trainer dreams of having. Dragon-types typically have amazing stats across the board, but they're rare and often difficult to train, plus they have to watch out for Fairy-types.

Super Effective Against	Weak To	Resists	Weak Against
Dragon	Dragon Fairy	Fire Grass Water Electric	Steel Fairy

FAIRY

The newest addition to the type roster, Fairy-types brought magic and balance to the Pokemon world and serve as the ultimate counter to the mighty Dragon-type. Fairy-types often have unique abilities that can completely change how battles play out.

Super Effective Against	Weak To	Resists	Weak Against
Dragon Fighting Dark	Poison Steel	Fighting Bug Dark	Fire Poison Steel

A TIMELINE OF EVOLUTION

From humble beginnings on the Game Boy to sprawling open-world adventures on modern consoles, Pokemon games have been capturing hearts and imagination for nearly three decades.

From black and white pixels to full 3D open world adventures, this timeline traces the incredible journey from 151 pocket monsters to over 1,000 species - and how each game built upon the last to create the ultimate monster-catching experience.

GENERATION I (1996-1999)

Total Pokemon: 151
Console: Nintendo Game Boy

- **Red & Blue (1998):** The games that started it all, These original adventures introduced the world to Pikachu, Charizard, and the dream of becoming a Pokemon Master. With 151 species to discover and a simple but addictive "gotta catch 'em all" formula, Red and Blue (Red and Green in Japan, released in 1996) created a gaming phenomenon that's still going strong today.

- **Yellow (1999):** Pikachu got the starring role in this enhanced version that followed the anime more closely. This was also the first game to feature all three original starters obtainable in a single playthrough!

> Gen I is the only generation where none of its game mascots are Legendary Pokemon.

GENERATION II (1999-2000)

New Pokemon: 100
Total Pokemon: 251
Console: Game Boy Color

- **Gold & Silver (1999):** Not only did these sequels add 100 new Pokemon, they also added day and night cycles, breeding, held items and two new types: Dark and Steel. Plus, you got to return to Kanto after beating the Elite Four, essentially giving you two games in one!

- **Crystal (2000):** The first in the series with animated sprites brought the Pokemon to life like never before. Crystal also introduced the ability to play as a female trainer and featured an expanded storyline focusing on the legendary Suicune.

> Gen II started the tradition of featuring the Legendary Pokemon as the cover art for main series games.

GENERATION III (2002-2005)

New Pokemon: 135
Total Pokemon: 386
Console: Game Boy Advance

- **Ruby & Sapphire (2002):** Moving to the Game Boy Advance meant new graphics and abilities, double battles, Pokemon contests, and secret bases. Oh, and 135 new species to add to the roster.

- **FireRed & LeafGreen (2004):** Red and Blue got a complete makeover with these remakes, proving the original formula was always an evergreen classic.

- **Emerald (2005):** This definitive version of Ruby/Sapphire added the Battle Frontier, a massive post-game challenge that tested every aspect of your training skills.

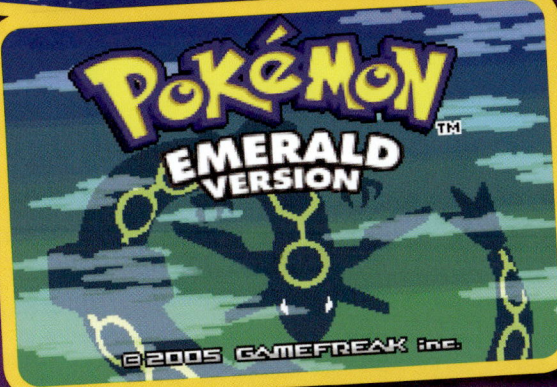

> Oddly enough, Gen III is the only generation that gives the player character both a mother and a father. Norman (the only PokéDad in the series, essentially) is also a Gym Leader!

Generation IV (2006-2009)

New Pokemon: 107
Total Pokemon: 493
Console: Nintendo DS

- **Diamond & Pearl (2006):** The first release for the DS, taking full advantage of touch controls and split screen. The Sinnoh region's mythology-heavy plot raised the stakes to legendary proportions.

- **Platinum (2008):** This enhanced version refined Diamond/Pearl's pacing and added the Distortion World. The Battle Frontier returned.

- **HeartGold & SoulSilver (2009):** These remakes brought Johto into the modern era. Having your Pokemon follow you on the overworld was amazing, and the post-game Kanto region was expanded with new content.

> Gen IV shared the newness love with older Pokemon, introducing the largest number of new evolutions for previous generation Pokemon (29).

Generation V (2010-2012)

New Pokemon: 156
Total Pokemon: 649
Console: Nintendo DS

- **Black & White (2010):** A bold experiment that restricted you to entirely new Pokemon until the post-game. These games featured the most mature storyline in the series, questioning the ethics of Pokemon training through the villainous Team Plasma.

- **Black 2 & White 2 (2012):** The first direct sequel in the series, set two years later with new areas, new gym leaders and new storylines.

> This generation brought the biggest increase in new Pokemon - 156 is even more than Gen I started out with.

GENERATION VI (2013-2014)

New Pokemon: 72
Total Pokemon: 721
Console: Nintendo 3DS

- **X & Y (2013):** The Nintendo 3DS brought 3D graphics to the series for the first time. Mega Evolution added a new strategic layer to battles, while the Fairy type was also introduced.

- **Omega Ruby & Alpha Sapphire (2014):** Hoenn got the full 3D treatment. The Delta Episode post-game story introduced the multiverse concept that would become crucial to later games.

> Gen VI is the only generation to not introduce a new pure Electric-type Pokemon.

GENERATION VII (2016-2017)

New Pokemon: 88
Total Pokemon: 809
Console: Nintendo 3DS

- **Sun & Moon (2016):** Gym Leaders? We don't need gym leaders! Island Trials and Totem Pokemon completely reimagined the Pokemon League structure. Z-Moves provided spectacular finishing moves, while Alolan forms gave us familiar Pokemon a new luau-look.

- **Ultra Sun & Ultra Moon (2017):** This marked the first time that new Pokemon were introduced mid-generation, bringing the running total from 802 to 807. It also provided an alternate storyline and new gameplay features.

> This was the first generation that didn't have a bicycle (RIP legend, we'll always have Cycling Road). Trainers just had to hop on their Pokemon to ride instead.

GENERATION VIII (2019-EARLY 2022)

New Pokemon: 96
Total Pokemon: 905
Console: Nintendo Switch

- **Sword & Shield (2019):** The Wild Area introduced semi-open world exploration to the series. Dynamax battles in massive stadiums made gym challenges feel like epic sporting events, while online raids encouraged cooperative play with friends..

- **Brilliant Diamond & Shining Pearl (2021):** Faithful recreations of the Sinnoh classics with modernized graphics and Elite Four rematches. The Underground was expanded into a massive multiplayer space for fossil hunting and secret base building.

- **Legends: Arceus (2022):** This prequel completely reimagined Pokemon gameplay with seamless catching, alpha Pokemon, and crafting mechanics! Set in ancient Sinnoh, it showed how humans and Pokemon first learned to coexist, featuring the first truly open-world Pokemon experience.

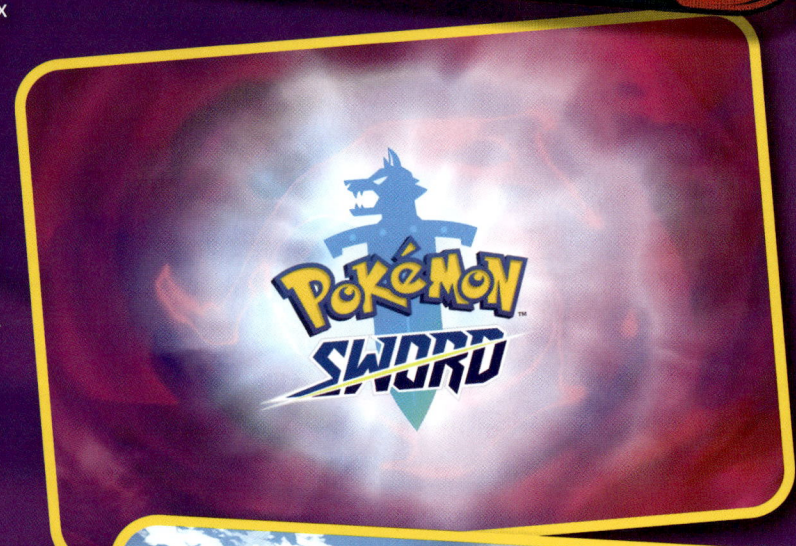

Gen VIII set a new record for the shortest gap between main game releases: just 70 days between Brilliant Diamond and Shining Pearl and Legends: Arceus!

GENERATION IX (2022-PRESENT)

New Pokemon: 120
Total Pokemon: 1025
Console: Nintendo Switch/ Nintendo Switch 2

- **Scarlet & Violet (2022):** We finally got full open-world exploration for the very first time. This game was bigger than ever, with three separate storylines that could be tackled in any order, and Terastalization adding a new crystal-powered twist to type match-ups.

- **The Teal Mask & The Indigo Disk (2023-2024):** These DLC expansions added new regions, with the return of beloved characters and the introduction of competitive academy battles.

- **Legends: Z-A (2025):** The latest entry (and likely last of Gen IX) is a sequel to 2022's Legends: Arceus. Mega Evolution returns as a central mechanic, allowing trainers to harness this powerful transformation in battles throughout the city.

Gen IX is the first generation since Gen V to introduce over 100 new Pokemon. It also has the most Pokemon with no possible evolutionary line (41).

POKEMON GO!

This mobile game revolution launched in 2016 and had millions of trainers wandering around parks, malls, and neighborhoods with their phones out, flicking Poké Balls at virtual creatures. Suddenly, everyone was a Pokemon trainer, and the real world became the ultimate Pokemon region.

HOW IT ALL WORKS

Pokemon GO uses your phone's GPS and camera to overlay Pokemon onto the real world through augmented reality (AR). Open the app, and wild Pokemon appear on your map based on your actual location. Water-types hang out near lakes and rivers, Grass-types love parks, and you'll find all sorts of surprises depending on where you live. The core gameplay is simple: walk around, find Pokemon, flick Poké Balls to catch them, and fill up your Pokedex.

SOCIAL REVOLUTION

Pokemon GO didn't just change gaming; it changed how people interact with their communities.

Raid Battles require teamwork to defeat powerful Pokemon that appear at Gyms. These battles bring strangers together - you'll find yourself coordinating with random players to take down a legendary Pokemon. Some of the strongest Pokemon in the game can only be caught through these collaborative efforts.

Switch out Pokemon during battle to utilize your battle party's different Charged Attacks.

The game also introduced Trading and Friendship systems. You can trade Pokemon with nearby players, and building friendships through regular interaction unlocks bonuses. Send gifts, battle together, and watch your friendship level grow for better rewards and trade discounts.

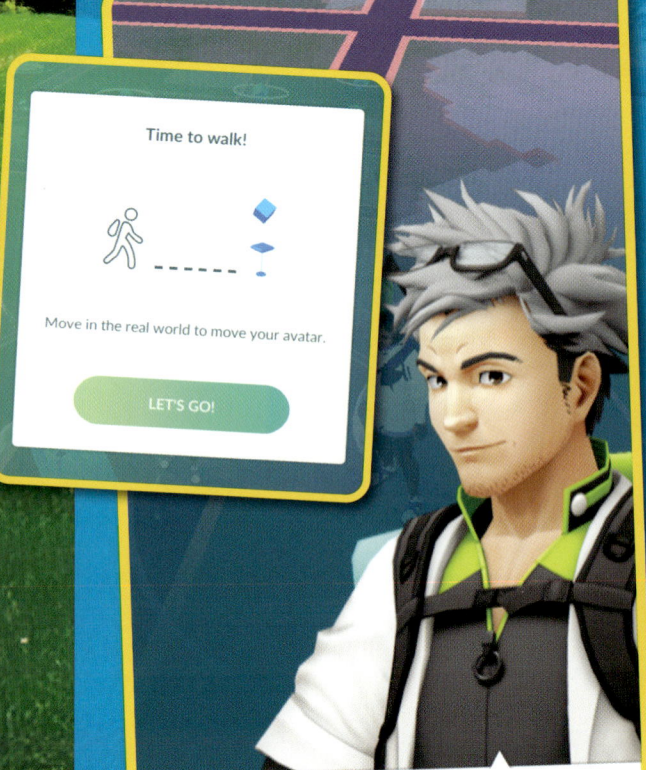

There's a Pokémon nearby!

TIPS FOR NEW TRAINERS

- **Start Smart, Not Hard:** Catch everything you see, even those annoying Pidgey and Rattata! Common Pokemon give valuable Stardust (the currency for powering up your team) and XP for leveling up. Spin every PokéStop you pass for free items, and don't hoard your resources early on – use those Poké Balls! You'll get more, we promise.

- **Master the Appraisal System:** Not all Pokemon are created equal! Use the in-game appraisal feature to check your Pokemon's Individual Values (IVs). Those three-star ratings mean you've got a keeper worth investing Stardust in. Combat Power (CP) shows current strength, but IVs determine potential.

REASONS TO RETURN: LATEST UPDATES

The biggest addition to hit Pokemon GO recently is the arrival of Dynamax and Gigantamax mechanics from Pokemon Sword & Shield! These supersized Pokemon can only be caught through Max Battles, a completely new type of raid found at Power Spots (not regular Gyms). Think regular raids were exciting? Wait until you see a Gigantamax Charizard towering over the battlefield!

You'll need up to three Dynamax Pokemon of your own to challenge these giants, creating a whole new collection and battle strategy meta. Recent months have seen Gigantamax versions of starter Pokemon like Rillaboom, Cinderace, and Inteleon making their debuts, with more promised throughout 2025. Max Mondays have become the new weekly event to look forward to!

- **Join the Community:** Find your local Pokemon GO Facebook group, Discord server, or Reddit community. Experienced trainers are surprisingly helpful and will share raid times, rare spawn locations, and insider tips. Plus, you'll need friends for trading and some research tasks!

Whether you're a returning trainer or just starting your GO journey, remember: the goal isn't just to catch 'em all – it's to get out there, meet people, and rediscover the world around you through the lens of Pokemon adventure. So grab your phone, lace up your walking shoes, and get ready to become the very best, like no one ever was!

LEGENDARY CROSSWORD

Some Pokemon are powerful. Some are rare. And then... there's Legendary. Each clue in this crossword points to one of these iconic Pokemon from across the regions - beasts of myth, masters of elements, and protectors of balance. Fill in the grid using the clues and see how many of these legends you can name.

CLUES

ACROSS

2. This Fairy-type Legendary's antlers resemble its game title. (7)

5. This draconic alien was responsible for the Darkest Day. (9)

7. This iron serpent comes from the future. (8)

8. This toxic dog is loyal to Pecharunt. (7)

9. This Electric-type beast was resurrected by Ho-Oh after the burning of Brass Tower. (6)

11. This elegant white dragon is part of the Tao trio. (8)

DOWN

1. This Legendary wolf is suited up for battle. (9)

3. This 2 million IQ Legendary is the OG. (6)

4. This hulking robot is the creator of the legendary giants. (9)

5. This lover girl may be more hate than love. (8)

6. This black beauty is a spectral steed. (9)

10. This cutie is a member of the lake guardians. (7)

32

WHO'S THAT POKEMON? 1

So you want to be a Pokemon Master? Every true champion knows their Pokedex inside out, and can identify any Pokemon at the drop of a hat. Can you identify the Pokemon from just its silhouette?

1.

2.

3.

CHECK OUT P62-63 FOR ANSWERS!

SPOT THE DIFFERENCE 1

Ah, there's nothing more beautiful than Pokemon in the wild. Can you spot seven differences between these two shots of Pokemon in their natural habitat?

BATTLE QUIZ

Okay, how closely were you paying attention to the Types guide a few pages back? Time to put you to the test. Who's likely to win if these Pokemon types face off?

1. Fire vs. Water

2. Fighting vs. Normal

3. Fairy vs. Dragon

4. Dragon vs. Steel

5. Water vs. Ground

6. Bug vs. Fire

7. Psychic vs. Poison

8. Electric vs. Flying

9. Ice vs. Grass

10. Ghost vs. Dark

CHECK OUT P62-63 FOR ANSWERS!

POKEDEX PECULIARITIES

We usually use the Pokedex as more of a catalogue to flex how many Pokemon we've caught, but it's actually a huge encyclopedia of knowledge on all the Pokemon out there - and sometimes it goes pretty deep. How closely have you looked at those entries? From child kidnapping, crushing spines and casual revenge arson, here are some Pokedex entries you might have missed...

- **Pokemon:** Drifloon
- **Pokedex Entry:** Sun

Stories go that it grabs the hands of small children and drags them away to the afterlife. It dislikes heavy children.

- **Pokemon:** Drampa
- **Pokedex Entry:** Ultra Sun

If a child it has made friends with is bullied, Drampa will find the bully's house and burn it to the ground.

- **Pokemon:** Bewear
- **Pokedex Entry:** Moon

This Pokemon has the habit of hugging its companions. Many Trainers have left this world after their spines were squashed by its hug.

- **Pokemon:** Gengar
- **Pokedex Entry:** Shield

It lays traps, hoping to steal the lives of those it catches. If you stand in front of its mouth, you'll hear your loved ones' voices calling out to you.

- **Pokemon:** Jellicent
- **Pokedex Entry:** Black

The fate of the ships and crew that wander into Jellicent's habitat: all sunken, all lost, all vanished.

- **Pokemon:** Mimikyu
- **Pokedex Entry:** Shield

There was a scientist who peeked under Mimikyu's old rag in the name of research. The scientist died of a mysterious disease.

- **Pokemon:** Gothitelle
- **Pokedex Entry:** Black 2

It can see the future from the movement of the stars. When it learns its Trainer's life span, it cries in sadness.

- **Pokemon:** Yamask
- **Pokedex Entry:** Black

Each of them carries a mask that used to be its face when it was human. Sometimes they look at it and cry.

- **Pokemon:** Froslass
- **Pokedex Entry:** Sun

When it finds humans or Pokemon it likes, it freezes them and takes them to its chilly den, where they become decorations.

KNOW THY ENEMY

Every great hero needs a worthy opponent, and the Pokemon world delivers some truly memorable villain teams. From world-conquering masterminds to vengeful outcasts, these groups have caused chaos across every region. Ready to meet the troublemakers? Let's dive into the wild world of Pokemon's most notorious organizations!

TEAM ROCKET

- **Game Appearances:** Red/Blue/Yellow, Gold/Silver/Crystal, FireRed/LeafGreen, HeartGold/SoulSilver
- **Anime Appearances:** Original series and beyond

The OG villains of the Pokemon world! Led by the mysterious Giovanni (who also moonlights as Viridian City's Gym Leader - hustle culture), Team Rocket wants to steal rare Pokemon and take over the world. Their motto? "Prepare for trouble, and make it double!" Their signature Pokemon include Persian, Meowth, and basically any Pokemon they can get their grubby hands on.

Fun fact: The bumbling Rocket duo Jessie and James from the anime series aren't actually in the games, but they've become more famous than most of the actual game villains! Giovanni eventually abandons Team Rocket after his defeat, leaving his son Silver to wrestle with daddy issues in Gold/Silver.

TEAM ROCKET captures POKéMON from around the world.▼

TEAM AQUA AND TEAM MAGMA

- **Game Appearances:** Ruby/Sapphire/Emerald, Omega Ruby/Alpha Sapphire
- **Anime Appearances:** Advanced Generation series

These weather-obsessed rivals from Hoenn are basically extreme environmentalists gone wrong. Team Aqua, led by Archie and his trusty Sharpedo, wants to expand the oceans to create a "perfect world" for Water Pokemon. Meanwhile, Team Magma's Maxie and his Camerupt dream of expanding the land for more living space. Spoiler alert: they both flop.

In Emerald, they actually team up at the end because they realize they've made a tiny mistake... like nearly destroying the world. Hey, Groudon and Kyogre don't mess around when it comes to climate change.

TEAM SKULL

- **Game Appearances:** Sun/Moon, Ultra Sun/Ultra Moon
- **Anime Appearances:** Sun & Moon series

Alola's "villain" team is less "world domination" and more "teenagers acting out." Led by Guzma, Team Skull are basically delinquents who cause trouble because they don't fit into Alola's island challenge system. Their signature Pokemon? Golisopod for Guzma, and lots of Zubat and Salandit for the grunts.

Most Team Skull members are just kids who failed the island trials and feel left behind by society. Even their "hideout" is a rundown mansion in Po Town. They're more likely to steal your lunch money than destroy the world.

TEAM STAR

- **Game Appearances:** Scarlet/Violet
- **Anime Appearances:** N/A

Paldea's Team Star flips the script entirely – they're the victims, not the villains! This group of students created their own "gang" to fight back against severe bullying at their academy. Each squad specializes in a different type (Fire, Dark, Poison, Fairy, Fighting) and is led by students who dropped out to escape their tormentors.

The real kicker? Their mysterious "Big Boss" Cassiopeia turns out to be... a lot closer to the player than initially thought (no spoilers here - you'll have to play the game yourself for this big reveal).

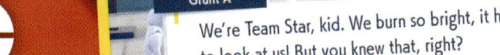

NEWLY NEFARIOUS

Move over, evil factions - there's a new nefarious organisation in town looking to steal some Pokemon, and they're looking good while doing so. Team Star? Wannabes. Team Skull? Try-hards. Team Rocket? Okay, well... absolute icons and that cannot be denied (I'm sorry for even bringing them up in this trio, truthfully).

Regardless, it's time for a new team to take on the antagonist role - your team! Design uniforms for the grunts and give them a name.

ROGUE ROLL CALL

Sure, the bad guy teams are all fun and games, but they're only exacting the rule of their nefarious leaders. Can you identify the main Pokemon antagonists from the clues below?

1. I once dreamed of segregating humans and Pokemon, but I had been brainwashed by my father into leading an evil faction. _____

2. I merged with Nihilego in my quest to find Ultra Beasts. _____

3. I am the most iconic criminal in Pokemon history - and I still find time to hold down a second job. _____

4. Everything I did was to protect Galar from the energy crisis. _____

5. I just wanted to make the world more beautiful, but I ended up discovering the secret to eternal life. _____

6. I was consumed by my research, corrupted by A.I. and reanimated by robots. _____

7. I want to be the only person in the whole world in possession of Pokemon. _____

8. I have no emotion. I have no spirit. I have no hope. _____

CHECK OUT P62-63 FOR ANSWERS!

BEST IN CLASS

There are more Pokemon than anyone can keep track of these days, but there are some that stand out from the pack for being the best in a certain field. Here are some of Pokemon's best in class.

To the surprise of exactly zero people, Ash's **Pikachu** is the Pokemon with the most screen time in the anime series, having clocked in for an appearance every single episode since it first started in 1997. Second place goes to Team Rocket's **Meowth**.

On the other end of the spectrum, the Pokemon with the least anime screen time (against the longest time they have been available - obviously the anime has to catch up to new Gens) is **Porygon**. This Pokemon was part of the Gen I rollout, but has only appeared once - and its one episode caused kids to be taken to hospital with epileptic seizures, so it was since pulled from airing and Porygon has essentially bore the blame by being banished ever since.

PORYGON

Stats wise, there are quite a few Pokemon tying for first place when it comes to the lightest. **Cosmog**, **Gastly**, **Haunter**, **Kartana** and **Flabébé** all weigh just 0.2 lbs, making them the lightest creatures in the Pokedex...

...So you might be surprised to learn that Cosmog's evolution, **Cosmoem**, is tied (with **Celesteela**) as the heaviest Pokemon on the roster, weighing in at a mammoth 999.9 kg. Cosmoem may look cute, but it's seriously dense. Needless to say, the jump from Cosmog to Cosmoem is the largest weight increase between evolutions, coming in at +999,8000%.

COSMOG

COSMOEM

The honour of tallest Pokemon goes to **Eternatus**, towering in at an intimidating 20 meters tall (that's as tall as ten standard sized sofas, by the way). And that's not even counting its Eternamax form, which grows to around 100 meters - as tall as the St. Paul's Cathedral.

ETERNATUS

For shortest Pokemon, there are quite a few that tie for first place. **Comfey**, **Cutiefly**, **Flabébé**, **Joltik** and **Sinistea** all measure in at just 20 centimeters. Well, one of them is a literal sentient teacup, so that shouldn't be all that surprising. What is surprising is that Cosmoem (yep, the same Pokemon that won heaviest at 999.9 kg) also measures in at 20 centimeters. Shortest and the heaviest, with quite the ratio too.

JOLTIK

CUTIEFLY

GIRATINA

ARCEUS

The oldest Pokemon is **Arceus**, who apparently predates existence itself. This shouldn't come as a massive shock, since Arceus is essentially the God of Pokemon and created the entire universe. Second place goes to the creation trio, **Palkia**, **Dialga** and **Giratina** (they really need to rethink that nickname, huh?).

EEVEE

EXPLOUD

The Pokemon with the most evolutions shouldn't come as a surprise to anyone: **Eevee**. Eevee dropped in the OG 150 Pokemon with three possible evolutions, but has since pushed that number to eight possible Eeveelutions (not our pun, so don't punish us for it) as the series grew - and that number is very likely to increase considering there's still a ton of types that don't have an Eevee representative yet.

The loudest Pokemon is undoubtedly **Whismur** and its evolutions **Loudred** and **Exploud**. It's said that Whismur's cry is over 100 decibels, and people from the past used Exploud's voice to communicate between distant cities. And Loudred has literal speakers for ears that are powerful enough to blow away a house, apparently. Menaces, the lot of them.

The race for the fastest title is certainly tight, but the indisputable winner is **Regieliki** from Gen VIII. Regieliki has a base speed of 200, which is just unmatched. Before Gen VIII came along, the longstanding champion speedster was **Deoxys**, who held the title since its introduction in Gen III.

PYUKUMUKU

If there's a fastest, then there's a slowest - and three Pokemon are crawling in to slowly grasp that honour. **Shuckle**, **Munchlax** and **Pyukumuku** all have a measly base speed of just 5, which (to put into perspective) is half the speed of a Pokemon that's literally stuck in a static treasure chest.

DEOXYS

MAZE MISSION

Can you make it through the maze to reach Pikachu?

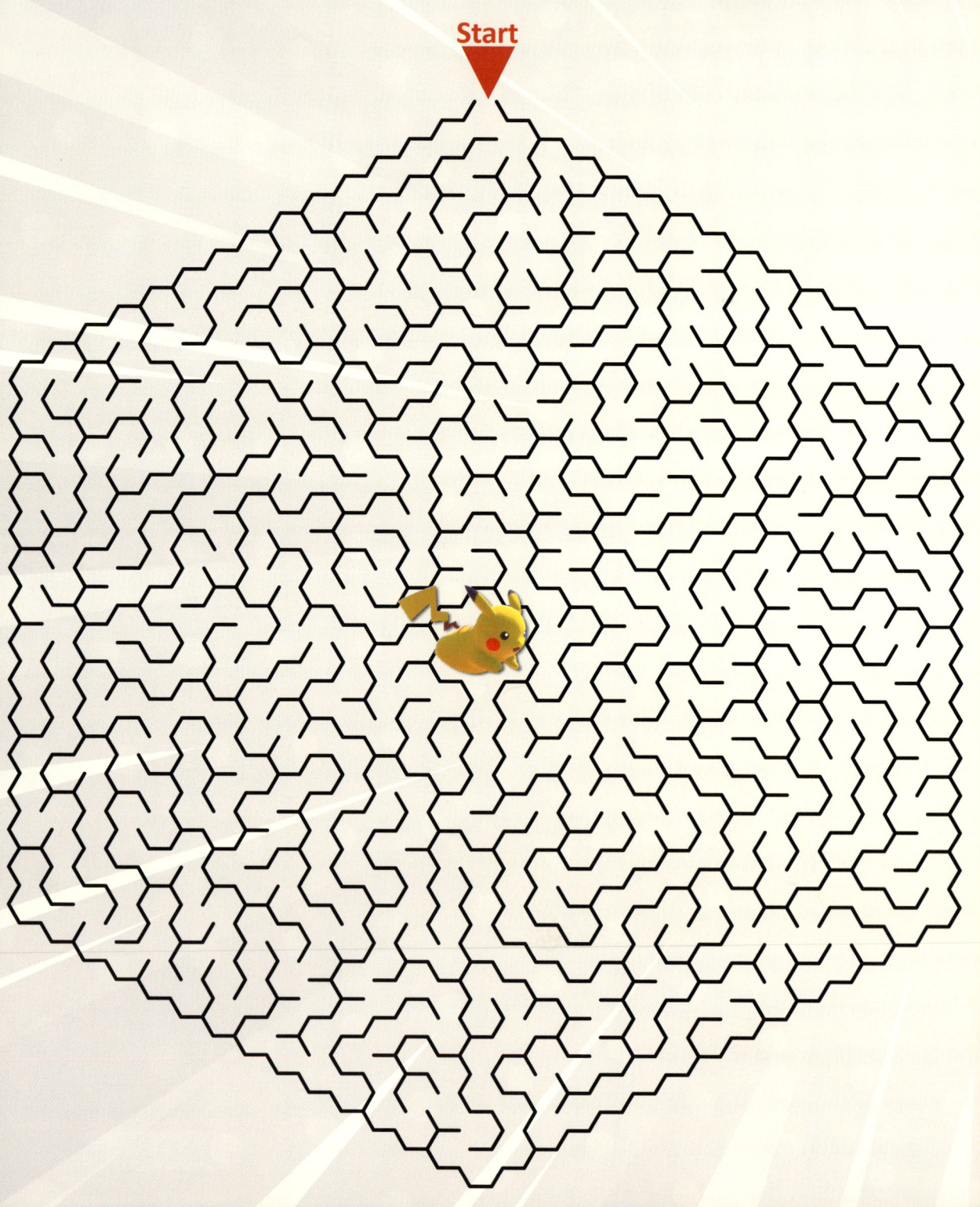

WHO'S THAT POKEMON? II

Your Pokedex is short-circuiting! *Sigh* I guess that's what we get for relying on tech too much, right? Time to test your biological database (i.e., your brain) to see if it can compete with the little red digibook. Can you identify the Pokemon from just its silhouette?

1

2

3

4

CHECK OUT P62-63 FOR ANSWERS!

WHOLESOME BEHAVIOUR

We've already covered some quite frankly disturbing Pokedex entries, but we wouldn't want you thinking the Pokedex is a horror story tome full of Creepypasta revelations behind your favourite friends. There's also a ton of wholesome and adorable entries with little facts and trivia that you wouldn't otherwise know.

- **Pokemon:** Blissey
- **Pokedex Entry:** Omega Ruby

Blissey senses sadness with its fluffy coat of fur. If it does so, this Pokemon will rush over to a sad person, no matter how far away, to share a Lucky Egg that brings a smile to any face.

- **Pokemon:** Goodra
- **Pokedex Entry:** Ultra Sun

It's very friendly toward people. If you grow close to it, Goodra will hug you with its sticky, slime-covered body. Don't get mad.

- **Pokemon:** Igglybuff
- **Pokedex Entry:** Ultra Sun

It's always practicing its singing because it wants to improve. Even when it's asleep, it keeps singing in its dreams!

- **Pokemon:** Murkow
- **Pokedex Entry:** Moon

Seen as a symbol of bad luck, it's generally disliked. Yet it gives presents — objects that sparkle or shine — to Trainers it's close to.

- **Pokemon:** Eldegoss
- **Pokedex Entry:** Sword

The seeds attached to its cotton fluff are full of nutrients. It spreads them on the wind so that plants and other Pokemon can benefit from them.

DEEP SEA SEARCH

Time for a deep dive into the sea! Can you find all of these aquatic Pokemon in the wordsearch below?

```
R J M F D Q W I L F I S H Y F H M W D Q B G S Q C
B S C I U M L N W I T G K U U C E P N U T W O H C
A H P S G M A N V B V E K N Z L Q X N U A Y Z J D
J A L Y O O M O X M F N N P W P N M A F Z F G Q B
B R O R R Z A M K Q C X B T W A I L O R D F U Y Y
D P C X E D T X W P R O G W A G H B H C W Z M V Q
U E T N B N S C M V A A T Z X C Z L Y X M E G M A
B D I O Y L I N Y C D Y H B J N O O M A S T A R M
C O L F S J D N H L I J V L R C K O Y W X O U M P
O S L F S B D V M A L Y S Q Q R T W L B X K F P L
R J E V X I H I B M Y R P P L Z I R C Z G F D O A
S H R D K Y V Q X P Y E K W H X I C H G N D M T E
O O Y Z B M E R T E N L K X B E C E I H P P Q W V
L P O V K I A O X R C I B R N S A Z N N M X F I S
A A N Q G C I V O L Y C K S R R I L C V W D V Z V
Z G D G W D K Y M I L A L P F Z M X H G Z N C Y I
I M I P N O P J P O H N U P W N K A O L A B U K K
Q A H B L N W L I T X T V S T R F G U P X H Y F Y
C N J U U T B R O I D H D E S F L B O H U K D T O
I T L E N B A V D O G Z I A A H C A S X Z T O X G
D I M L T T W X R U E T S D G U E T P S E F C X R
T N V W X V A Z B X J D C R S P R X A N O A W Y E
N E P Z W K S I C Q D E M A G I I Q X Z M T N C D
Z D H B F Y N M L E N Z G W Z J C A R V A N H A J
D I C Q P C F W U L L B P U G G K N L A N T U R N
```

Tentacool	Corsola	Wailord	Relicanth
Seadra	Mantine	Cradily	Spheal
Omastar	Chinchou	Clamperl	Luvdisc
Lanturn	Octillery	Gorebyss	Huntail
Qwilfish	Sharpedo	Carvanha	Kyogre

SPOT THE DIFFERENCE II

Welcome to the Pokemon Center! Can you spot the eight differences between these two shots?

SANDS SCRAMBLE

Time to turn our eye to the scorching, sweeping sands. Can you unscramble and identify these Pokemon that live in the desert? We've given you the first letter as a clue.

1. SDNEWAHSR

2. TCRPNHAI

3. CEACAN

4. HDPNIWOOP

5. MUNZABZID

6. HIELOKLIS

7. CRECNAUT

8. LCOANRYC

9. KHNAAGANSK

10. TAYRNRITA

CHECK OUT P62-63 FOR ANSWERS!

PIKACHU PROFILE

Move over, Mickey, there's a new iconic mouse in town - and this one can fry anyone who objects. Pikachu is arguably the world's most recognized character, appearing everywhere you look since 1996. Your local toy store, plastered on the side of airplanes flying overhead, printed on the back of official currency coins - this yellow, rosy-cheeked rodent has somehow conquered the world.

Profile
Height: 0.4m (1'04")
Weight: 6.0kg (13.2 lbs)
Type: Electric
First Appeared: 1996 in Japan

WHAT'S IN A NAME?

Pikachu's name comes from a mix of two Japanese onomatopoeia: ピカピカ pikapika, the sound of something sparking with electricity, and チューチュ chuchu, the squeaky sound a mouse makes.

BEGINNING SKETCHES

Pikachu's original design wasn't based on a mouse; its first inspiration was actually a squirrel, according to designer Atsuko Nishida. The lightning bolt tail and back stripes were added later to bring the design to life, while the black-tipped ears are a leftover detail from an early version that resembled a daifuku, a soft Japanese dessert. Some fans also think Pikachu has a hint of viscacha, a desert-dwelling rodent related to chinchillas.

In 2008, a team of Japanese researchers discovered a new protein that helps transmit electrical signals from the eyes to the brain - and named it pikachurin in honor of Pikachu's lightning-fast reflexes.

Pikachu is the most represented Pokemon in the TGC, with over 200 unique cards.

PIKA PIKA!

Pikachu made its big splash as the co-lead of the Pokemon animated series. The show was a success from Day 1, and has since been broadcast in nearly 200 countries and territories (pretty much every nation on Earth, and that isn't exaggerating).

Even though the show has been translated into dozens of languages, Pikachu's signature "Pika Pika!" remains the same worldwide - performed by voice actress Ikue Ōtani since 1997. She even took on the role in the games for X and Y and Legends: Arceus.

HIS & HERS

For a long time, Pokemon games showed gender using the male (♂) and female (♀) symbols on screen, but didn't include many visual differences (except for Nidoran♂ and Nidoran♀).

That all changed in Diamond and Pearl, when more Pokemon began getting physical differences based on gender. Pikachu got a cute update: female Pikachu have a small notch in their tail that makes it look heart-shaped.

(ALMOST) PERSON OF THE YEAR

Time magazine ranked Pikachu as the "second best person of the year" in 1999. Pause. Let's examine that for a second: a major global news outlet put a cartoon mouse in their annual rankings alongside celebrities and world leaders. In second place. Prince William came in 10th.

THE CREATOR: ARCEUS

Arceus isn't just another legendary - it's the mythical deity that shaped the entire Pokemon universe from nothing but chaos. Known as the Original One, this Alpha Pokemon stands at the very top of the legendary hierarchy, making powerhouses like Mewtwo and Rayquaza look like chumps. If you've ever wondered who's responsible for your favorite Pokemon existing in the first place, you're looking at 'em.

Profile
Type: Normal (kinda, it's complicated)
Height: 10'6" (3.2 m)
Weight: 705.5 lbs (320 kg)
First Appearance: Diamond/Pearl

THE CREATION STORY

According to Sinnoh mythology, Arceus emerged from an egg in a place where there was nothing; not even time or space (please don't ask where the egg came from). With its incredible power, Arceus created Dialga to control time, Palkia to govern space, and Giratina to rule antimatter (a job she promptly got fired from, so family drama exists even at cosmic creator levels it seems).

But Arceus didn't stop there. It then created the physical world itself, shaping continents and oceans before finally resting. Some legends even suggest that every single Pokemon species can trace its lineage back to Arceus in some way.

MULTITYPE MASTER

So here's where it gets complicated. Arceus is unique in its Multitype ability - it can change its type to match whatever Plate it's holding. No other Pokemon has this level of adaptability. Makes sense for it to be able to rewrite the very rules of type effectiveness.

Despite being the literal creator of the universe, Arceus is still happy to chill in a Pokéball. Okay, sure, a Master Ball, but still.

Arceus is said to have 1,000 arms. Huh - just looks like 4, right? Well, what we see is just an avatar - Arceus' true form is beyond our measly human comprehension.

Did you know that the Pokemon Unown is believed to be sentient fragments of Arceus' power?

BATTLE TYPE CHEAT SHEET

Pokemon Type Effectiveness

Vulnerable To   Strong Against

POKEMON FUN FACTS

For over 25 years, Pokemon has captured hearts around the world, evolving from a simple Game Boy adventure into a global phenomenon that spans games, shows, movies, and countless friendships. Whether you're a seasoned trainer who's been catching 'em all since the beginning or a newer fan ready to dive deeper into this incredible world, there's always something new to discover in the ever-expanding Pokemon universe.

- Pokemon is actually a portmanteau of the Japanese name, Poketto Monsutā, which translates to "Pocket Monster" in English.

- Wildly enough, Ash's partner in crime was originally supposed to be Clefairy. Sure, Clefairy is cute and fluffy too, but it's difficult to imagine a world where Pikachu wasn't front and center of all faces of the franchise.

- We've always known the lead of the Pokemon anime to Ash Ketchum, but he's not known as that worldwide. In Japan, his name is Satoshi - named after the Pokemon creator and Game Freak head honcho, Satoshi Tajiri. Ash's OG rival Gary is called Shigeru in Japanese, the same name as the creator of Mario and Legend of Zelda series, Shigeru Miyamoto.

- Water has become the most common Pokemon type of all eighteen types, but that reign only started from Gen II. When Gen I was first introduced, Poison was the most common type. In fact, there were more Poison types in Gen I than there have been introduced in all the subsequent Gens combined.

- Ever wondered why the move Splash doesn't actually... splash any water? Well, the Japanese word for the move can mean both "splash" and "hop". Since we don't have a word as versatile, the translators went with Splash, despite the fact the move can be used by non-Water-types, and doesn't work under Gravity.

- Pikachu was printed on IRL money. Everyone's favourite yellow electric mouse made the back of a one dollar coin for the South Pacific island of Niue back in 2001.

- The first Pokemon designed by the team was not Bulbasaur (despite it being first in the Pokedex), or Pikachu (the inarguable first and enduring mascot of the series) - it was Rhydon (#112 in the Pokedex). Ken Sugimori - the primary designer at Pokemon - said that Lapras (#112) and Clefairy (#35) were some other early additions.

- Pokemon Gold and Silver were intended to be the final Pokemon games. Yes, you read that right: the series was going to end way back in 1999. Pokemon Company CEO Tsunekazu Ishihara said that he intended to move on from Pokemon after Gold and Silver, but the first entries to Gen II sold so well that it's fair to say some minds were changed.

- Speaking of designers, did you know that James Turner was the first westerner to officially join the team and design Pokemon? From 2010, his designs like Vanillite, Trevenant and Guzzlord have been included in the series.

- The Pokemon series holds quite a few Guinness World Records. It holds the title for longest-running anime series based on a video game, the fastest mobile game to gross $100 million (Pokemon Go) and perhaps most impressively: the best-selling role-playing game of all time.

UP CLOSE & PERSONAL

Can you work out which Pokemon is up close under the spotlight?

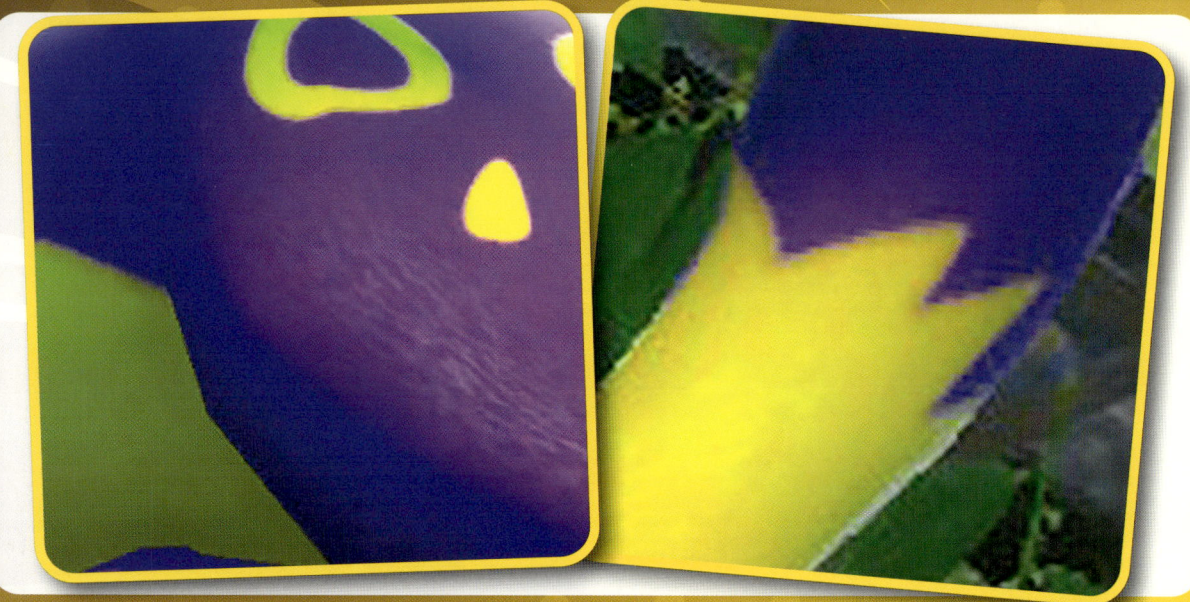

1

2

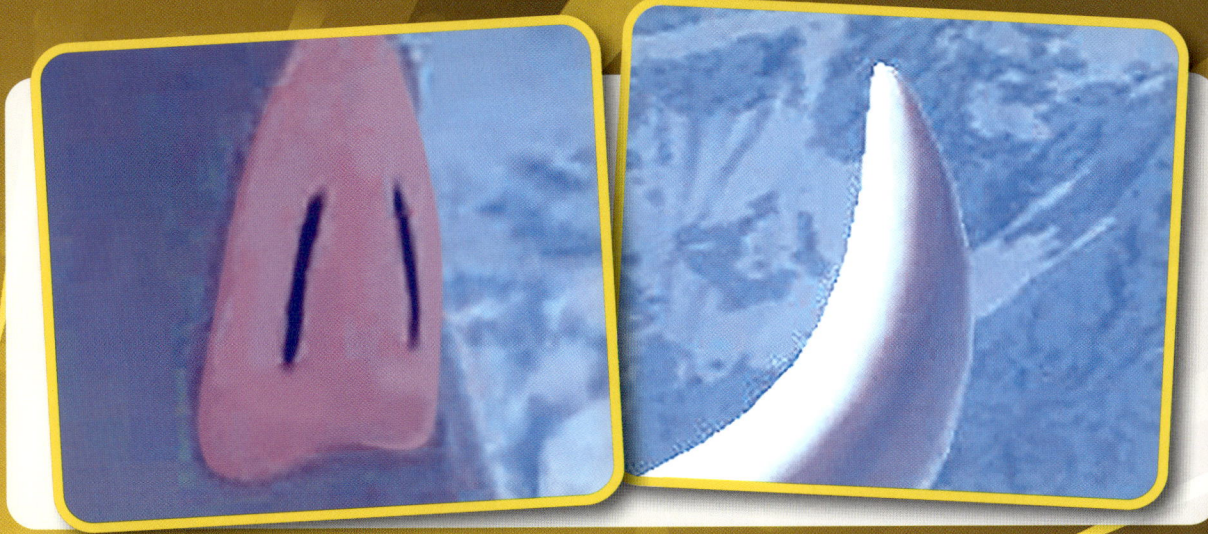

3

4

5

CHECK OUT P62-63 FOR ANSWERS!

POKEMON TCG

Picture this: it's 1996 in Japan, and Pokemon video games are taking the country by storm. Kids are obsessed with catching, training, and battling their digital monsters. Then someone had a brilliant idea: what if we could bring that same excitement to the real world with actual cards you could hold, trade, and collect?

THE BEGINNING

It all started in Japan in 1996, when Media Factory released the first Pokemon card game set, known as "Base Set." The Pokemon Trading Card Game was originally published in Japan in October 1996 by Media Factory, and it didn't take long for the rest of the world to catch on.

The timing was perfect: the anime was airing on TV, the digital games were flying off shelves, and now kids could physically own their favorite Pokemon. It was the perfect storm that created one of the most successful card games in history.

HOW TO PLAY

It's a pretty simple concept to boil down: each player builds a deck of 60 cards featuring their favourite Pokemon, plus trainer cards and energy cards to power their attacks. The goal is simple - knock out your opponent's Pokemon to collect prize cards, and the first player to collect all their prizes wins.

The strategy comes from building a deck that works well together, managing your energy, and timing your attacks perfectly. Matches typically last 20-30 minutes, and there's an official tournament scene where players compete for prizes and the world champion title.

FROM CARDBOARD TO GOLD

Those Pokemon cards that parents used to find scattered around the house? Some of them are now worth more than sports cars.

The most valuable Pokemon card is the 1998 Pokemon Japanese Promo Illustrator and it was sold for $5,275,000 in 2021. That's right: five million dollars for a single piece of cardboard with Pikachu drawn on it. Logan Paul's copy of this card is the only existing GEM-MT 10 copy that is known. He now holds the Guinness World Record for the most expensive Pokemon card ever sold.

But it's not just that one legendary card. The entire vintage card market has exploded over the past few years. Cards that sold for $50 in 2019 are now selling for thousands. A pristine first-edition Charizard (a holy grail for collectors) regularly sells for over $100,000.

PLAY TODAY

While vintage cards grab the headlines, the modern Pokemon TCG is healthier than ever. New sets are released every few months, each bringing fresh artwork, new Pokemon, and innovative game mechanics. Modern competitive play is more strategic and balanced than ever, with official tournaments offering substantial prize pools and scholarship opportunities for younger players.

So you want to start playing the Pokemon TCG? Start out with a Theme Deck or Battle Academy Box - these come with everything you need to learn the game. Happy trading!

Want to find out more? Check out the Pokemon TGC's official website at https://tcg.pokemon.com/ for cards, live match streaming and how to play guides.

THE BIG POKEMON QUIZ

It all comes down to this. This final quiz is your chance to show off everything you know about the world of Pokemon: battles, evolutions, types, Legendaries… When we say everything, we mean everything. Think you've got what it takes to be a true Pokemon Champion?

1. Who is the very first Pokemon in the National Pokedex?

2. Which real world country served as inspiration for Galar?

3. What is the one Pokemon-type that isn't represented in the Legendary line-up?

4. Which region has no gyms or gym leaders?

5. Which item can prevent a Pokemon from evolving?

6. Which move allows a Pokemon to mimic its opponent?

7. Who is the familiar face at every Pokécenter?

8. Which region has a Legendary trio of pups?

9. What type is the Eeveelution Umbreon?

10. Which Pokemon has the highest base stats in Gen I?

11. How many badges do trainers need to challenge the Pokemon League?

12. Which Legendary is known as the Guardian of the Sea?

13. What is the base friendship level of most Pokemon?

14. Which mythical Pokemon can travel through time?

15. How many arms does Machamp have?

16. What year was Pokemon first released in Japan?

17. How heavy is Cosmoem?

18. What item can wake a sleeping Snorlax?

19. Who is the starter Fire-type for Hoenn?

20. Who is the son of Team Plasma Leader Ghetsis?

21. Which Generation introduced the Fairy-type?

22. What is the maximum number of Pokemon a player can have in their party?

23. What's the one game in the main series where the trainer has a father?

24. What colour is a Shiny Charizard?

25. Which Pokemon is revived from an Old Amber fossil?

26. How much HP does a Hyper Potion restore?

27. Which Pokemon was the first to receive a Mega Evolution?

28. In the anime, what is the first Pokemon that Ash actually catches?

29. What is the only Pokemon that can learn every TM and HM move?

30. Which antagonist is the mother of Gladion and Lillie?

CHECK OUT P62-63 FOR ANSWERS!

ANSWERS

32: Legendary Crossword

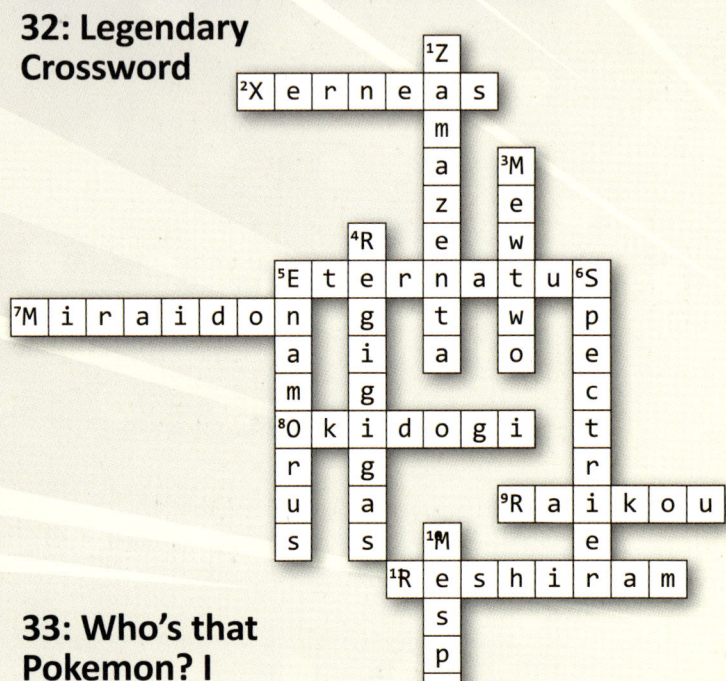

33: Who's that Pokemon? I
1. Espeon
2. Shinx
3. Vanillux

35: Battle Quiz
1. Water
2. Fighting
3. Fairy
4. Steel
5. Water
6. Fire
7. Psychic
8. Electric
9. Ice
10. Dark

41: Rogue Roll Call
1. N
2. Lusamine
3. Giovanni
4. Rose
5. Lysandre
6. Sada/Turo
7. Ghetsis
8. Cyrus

34: Spot the Difference I